I0607717

TOUGH TIMES

don't last

TOUGH TEAMS DO

"If you never give up you become unbeatable, just keep going!"

"I JUST WANTED TO LET YOU KNOW THAT HAVING YOU ON OUR TEAM MAKES ALL THE DIFFERENCE. THANKS FOR ALL YOU DO"

NEVER GIVE UP
KEEP MOVING
FORWARD

"Believe in miracles but above all believe in yourself!"

Date: /   /

_____

_____

_____

_____

_____

_____

_____

_____

_____

_____

_____

_____

_____

_____

_____

_____

_____

THINGS TO BE GRATEFUL FOR TODAY

"Let your dreams be as big as your desire to succeed"

Date: /   /

_____

_____

_____

_____

_____

_____

_____

_____

_____

_____

_____

_____

_____

_____

_____

_____

_____

THINGS TO BE GRATEFUL FOR TODAY

"Never downgrade your dreams, reach for the stars and believe in your self power"

Date: / /

THINGS TO BE GRATEFUL FOR TODAY

Date: /   /

THINGS TO BE GRATEFUL FOR TODAY

> *"Never be afraid to start something new, if you fail it is just temporary, if you believe and persist you will succeed"*

Date: /   /

_____

_____

_____

_____

_____

_____

_____

_____

_____

_____

_____

_____

_____

_____

_____

_____

_____

THINGS TO BE GRATEFUL FOR TODAY

"Your driving force and your power lies within you and the size of your dreams, never give up!"

Date: /   /

_____

_____

_____

_____

_____

_____

_____

_____

_____

_____

_____

_____

_____

_____

_____

_____

_____

THINGS TO BE GRATEFUL FOR TODAY

> *"Wherever you go, go with all your heart."*
> *- Confucius*

Date: /   /

_____
_____
_____
_____
_____
_____
_____
_____
_____
_____
_____
_____
_____
_____
_____
_____
_____

THINGS TO BE GRATEFUL FOR TODAY

"Never Ever Give Up"

Date: /   /

THINGS TO BE GRATEFUL FOR TODAY

Date: /   /

_____

_____

_____

_____

_____

_____

_____

_____

_____

_____

_____

_____

_____

_____

_____

_____

_____

THINGS TO BE GRATEFUL FOR TODAY

"Never give up, keep going no matter what!"

Date: / /

_____

_____

_____

_____

_____

_____

_____

_____

_____

_____

_____

_____

_____

_____

_____

_____

_____

THINGS TO BE GRATEFUL FOR TODAY

"Start where you are and take chances"

Date: /   /

_____

_____

_____

_____

_____

_____

_____

_____

_____

_____

_____

_____

_____

_____

_____

_____

_____

THINGS TO BE GRATEFUL FOR TODAY

"keep taking chances - make life a beautiful experience and never give up"

Date: /   /

THINGS TO BE GRATEFUL FOR TODAY

"Life isn't about finding yourself. Life is about creating yourself." - George Bernard Shaw

Date: /   /

THINGS TO BE GRATEFUL FOR TODAY

> *"Change your life today. Don't gamble on the future, act now, without delay."* — Simone de Beauvoir

Date: /   /

_____

_____

_____

_____

_____

_____

_____

_____

_____

_____

_____

_____

_____

_____

_____

_____

THINGS TO BE GRATEFUL FOR TODAY

"Keep your motivation and your momentum with a new goal every day!"

Date: /   /

_____

_____

_____

_____

_____

_____

_____

_____

_____

_____

_____

_____

_____

_____

_____

_____

THINGS TO BE GRATEFUL FOR TODAY

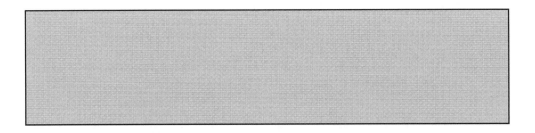

"Aim for the stars to keep your dreams alive"

Date: /   /

_____
_____
_____
_____
_____
_____
_____
_____
_____
_____
_____
_____
_____
_____
_____
_____
_____

THINGS TO BE GRATEFUL FOR TODAY

"When life gives you lemons, add a little gin and tonic"

Date: /   /

_____

_____

_____

_____

_____

_____

_____

_____

_____

_____

_____

_____

_____

_____

_____

THINGS TO BE GRATEFUL FOR TODAY

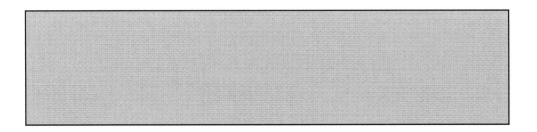

"There are no limits to what you can achieve if you believe in your dreams"

Date: /   /

_____

_____

_____

_____

_____

_____

_____

_____

_____

_____

_____

_____

_____

_____

_____

_____

_____

_____

THINGS TO BE GRATEFUL FOR TODAY

"When you feel you are defeated, just remember, you have the power to move on, it is all in your mind"

Date: /   /

THINGS TO BE GRATEFUL FOR TODAY

"Don't just dream your dreams, make them happen!"

Date: /   /

_____

THINGS TO BE GRATEFUL FOR TODAY

"Opportunity comes to those who never give up"

Date: /   /

_____

_____

_____

_____

_____

_____

_____

_____

_____

_____

_____

_____

_____

_____

_____

_____

THINGS TO BE GRATEFUL FOR TODAY

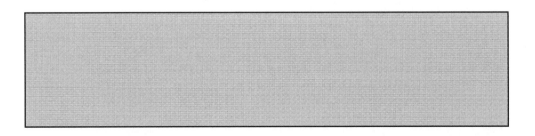

Date: /   /

THINGS TO BE GRATEFUL FOR TODAY

> *"Always aim for bigger goals, they have the power to keep you motivated"*

Date: /   /

_____

_____

_____

_____

_____

_____

_____

_____

_____

_____

_____

_____

_____

_____

_____

THINGS TO BE GRATEFUL FOR TODAY

> *"Success is not a place or a destination, it is a way of thinking while always having a new goal in mind"*

Date: /   /

THINGS TO BE GRATEFUL FOR TODAY

> *"Every achievement starts with
> a dream and a goal in mind"*

Date: /   /

_____

_____

_____

_____

_____

_____

_____

_____

_____

_____

_____

_____

_____

_____

_____

_____

_____

THINGS TO BE GRATEFUL FOR TODAY

"Change the world one dream at a time, believe in your dreams"

Date: / /

_____

_____

_____

_____

_____

_____

_____

_____

_____

_____

_____

_____

_____

_____

_____

_____

THINGS TO BE GRATEFUL FOR TODAY

"Never loose confidence in your dreams, there will be obstacles and defeats, but you will always win if you persist"

Date: /   /

THINGS TO BE GRATEFUL FOR TODAY

""*Never wait for someone else to validate your existence, you are the creator of your own destiny*"

Date: /   /

THINGS TO BE GRATEFUL FOR TODAY

"Dreams are the energy that power your life"

Date: /   /

THINGS TO BE GRATEFUL FOR TODAY

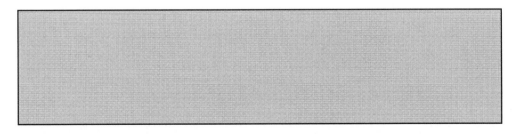

"Dreams make things happen, nothing is impossible as long as you believe." - Anonymous

Date: / /

_____
_____
_____
_____
_____
_____
_____
_____
_____
_____
_____
_____
_____
_____
_____
_____
_____

THINGS TO BE GRATEFUL FOR TODAY

"Always dream big and follow your heart"

Date: /   /

THINGS TO BE GRATEFUL FOR TODAY

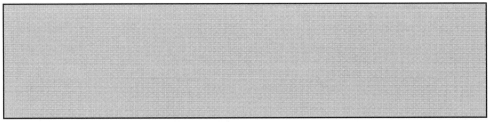

"Never stop dreaming." - Anonymous

Date: /   /

_____

_____

_____

_____

_____

_____

_____

_____

_____

_____

_____

_____

_____

_____

_____

_____

_____

THINGS TO BE GRATEFUL FOR TODAY

> *"Everything you dream is possible as long as you believe in yourself"*

Date: /   /

_____

_____

_____

_____

_____

_____

_____

_____

_____

_____

_____

_____

_____

_____

_____

_____

_____

THINGS TO BE GRATEFUL FOR TODAY

"Dream big, it's the first step to success" - Anonymous

Date: /   /

THINGS TO BE GRATEFUL FOR TODAY

"A successful person is someone that understands temporary defeat as a learning process, never give up!"

Date: /   /

THINGS TO BE GRATEFUL FOR TODAY

"Motivation comes from working on our dreams and from taking action to achieve our goals"

Date: /   /

_____

_____

_____

_____

_____

_____

_____

_____

_____

_____

_____

_____

_____

_____

_____

_____

_____

_____

_____

THINGS TO BE GRATEFUL FOR TODAY

> *"Dreams are the foundation to our imagination and success"*

Date: /   /

_____

_____

_____

_____

_____

_____

_____

_____

_____

_____

_____

_____

_____

_____

_____

_____

THINGS TO BE GRATEFUL FOR TODAY

> *"Your mission in life should be to thrive and not merely survive"*

Date: /   /

_____
_____
_____
_____
_____
_____
_____
_____
_____
_____
_____
_____
_____
_____
_____
_____
_____
_____
_____
_____

THINGS TO BE GRATEFUL FOR TODAY

"Doing what you believe in, and going after your dreams will only result in success." - Anonymous

Date: /   /

_____

_____

_____

_____

_____

_____

_____

_____

_____

_____

_____

_____

_____

_____

_____

_____

THINGS TO BE GRATEFUL FOR TODAY

"The right time to start something new is now"

Date: /   /

_____

_____

_____

_____

_____

_____

_____

_____

_____

_____

_____

_____

_____

_____

_____

_____

_____

THINGS TO BE GRATEFUL FOR TODAY

> *"Be brave, fight for what you believe in and make your dreams a reality."* - Anonymous

Date: /   /

_____
_____
_____
_____
_____
_____
_____
_____
_____
_____
_____
_____
_____
_____
_____
_____
_____

THINGS TO BE GRATEFUL FOR TODAY

Date: /   /

THINGS TO BE GRATEFUL FOR TODAY

"Let your dreams be bigger than your fears and your actions louder than your words." - Anonymous

Date: /   /

_____

_____

_____

_____

_____

_____

_____

_____

_____

_____

_____

_____

_____

_____

_____

_____

_____

THINGS TO BE GRATEFUL FOR TODAY

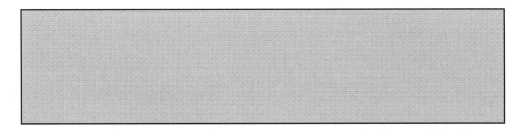

"Always keep moving forward to keep your balance, if you stop dreaming you will fall"

Date: /   /

THINGS TO BE GRATEFUL FOR TODAY

"Start every day with a goal in mind and make it happen with your actions"

Date: /   /

THINGS TO BE GRATEFUL FOR TODAY

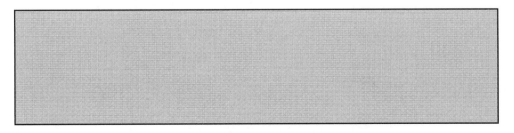

"Dream. Believe. Create. Succeed" - Anonymous

Date: /   /

THINGS TO BE GRATEFUL FOR TODAY

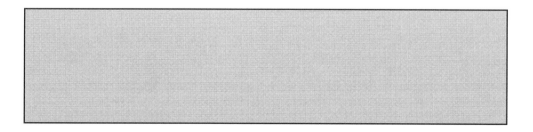

> *"You are never to old to set new goals and achieve them, keep on dreaming!"*

Date: / /

_____

_____
_____
_____
_____
_____
_____
_____
_____
_____
_____
_____
_____
_____
_____
_____
_____
_____
_____

THINGS TO BE GRATEFUL FOR TODAY

> *"If you have big dreams you will always have big reasons to wake up every day"*

Date: /   /

_____

_____

_____

_____

_____

_____

_____

_____

_____

_____

_____

_____

_____

_____

THINGS TO BE GRATEFUL FOR TODAY

"Difficulties are nothing more than opportunities in disguise, keep on trying and you will succeed"

Date: /   /
_____

_____

_____

_____

_____

_____

_____

_____

_____

_____

_____

_____

_____

_____

_____

_____

THINGS TO BE GRATEFUL FOR TODAY

Date: /   /

THINGS TO BE GRATEFUL FOR TODAY

> *"Always have a powerful reason to wake up every new morning, set goals and follow your dreams"*

Date: /   /

_____

_____

_____

_____

_____

_____

_____

_____

_____

_____

_____

_____

_____

_____

_____

THINGS TO BE GRATEFUL FOR TODAY

"Use failure as a motivation tool not as a sign of defeat"

Date: /   /

THINGS TO BE GRATEFUL FOR TODAY

*"Never let your dreams die for fear of failure,
defeat is just temporary; your dreams are your power"*

Date: /   /

_____

_____

_____

_____

_____

_____

_____

_____

_____

_____

_____

_____

_____

_____

_____

_____

THINGS TO BE GRATEFUL FOR TODAY

"A failure is a lesson, not a loss. It is a temporary and sometimes necessary detour, not a dead end"

Date: /   /

THINGS TO BE GRATEFUL FOR TODAY

"Have faith in the future but above all in yourself"

Date: /   /

_____

_____

_____

_____

_____

_____

_____

_____

_____

_____

_____

_____

_____

_____

_____

_____

THINGS TO BE GRATEFUL FOR TODAY

"Those who live in the past limit their future"
- Anonymous

Date: /   /

_____

_____

_____

_____

_____

_____

_____

_____

_____

_____

_____

_____

_____

_____

_____

_____

THINGS TO BE GRATEFUL FOR TODAY

"Your future is created by what you do today not tomorrow" - Anonymous

Date: /   /
_____

_____
_____
_____
_____
_____
_____
_____
_____
_____
_____
_____
_____
_____
_____
_____
_____
_____

THINGS TO BE GRATEFUL FOR TODAY

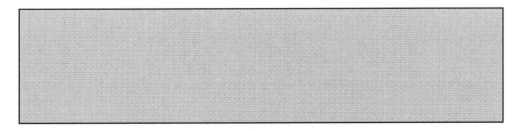

"Never let your doubt blind your goals, for your future lies in your ability, not your failure" — Anonymous

Date: / /

THINGS TO BE GRATEFUL FOR TODAY

> *"Don't go into something to test the waters,*
> *go into things to make waves" — Anonymous*

Date: /   /

THINGS TO BE GRATEFUL FOR TODAY

"Laughter is the shock absorber that softens and minimizes the bumps of life" — Anonymous

Date: /   /

THINGS TO BE GRATEFUL FOR TODAY

Date: /   /

_____

_____

_____

_____

_____

_____

_____

_____

_____

_____

_____

_____

_____

_____

_____

_____

_____

THINGS TO BE GRATEFUL FOR TODAY

Date: /   /

THINGS TO BE GRATEFUL FOR TODAY

"If you want to feel rich, just count all the things you have that money can't buy" — Anonymous

Date: /   /

THINGS TO BE GRATEFUL FOR TODAY

> *"Never give up on a dream just because of the time it will take to accomplish it. The time will pass anyway."* — Anonymous

Date: /   /

THINGS TO BE GRATEFUL FOR TODAY

"I am never a failure until I begin blaming others"
- Anonymous

Date: /   /

_____

_____

_____

_____

_____

_____

_____

_____

_____

_____

_____

_____

_____

_____

_____

_____

_____

_____

THINGS TO BE GRATEFUL FOR TODAY

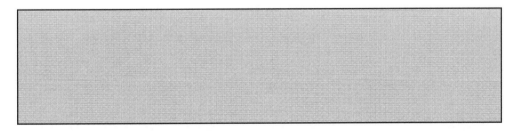

"Your only limitation is your imagination" — *Anonymous*

Date: /   /

_____

_____

_____

_____

_____

_____

_____

_____

_____

_____

_____

_____

_____

_____

_____

THINGS TO BE GRATEFUL FOR TODAY

> *"Some pursue success and happiness – others create it"* — Anonymous

Date: /   /

THINGS TO BE GRATEFUL FOR TODAY

> *"Anything worth doing is worth doing well"*
> *— Anonymous*

Date: /   /

_____

_____

_____

_____

_____

_____

_____

_____

_____

_____

_____

_____

_____

_____

THINGS TO BE GRATEFUL FOR TODAY

"It's better to have an impossible dream than no dream at all." – Anonymous

Date: /   /

_____

_____
_____
_____
_____
_____
_____
_____
_____
_____
_____
_____
_____
_____
_____
_____
_____
_____
_____
_____

THINGS TO BE GRATEFUL FOR TODAY

"Never let defeat have the last word" — Anonymous

Date: /   /

THINGS TO BE GRATEFUL FOR TODAY

"The winner always has a plan; The loser always has an excuse" — Anonymous

Date: /   /

THINGS TO BE GRATEFUL FOR TODAY

> *"There is no elevator to success.*
> *You have to take the stairs"* — Anonymous

Date: /   /

THINGS TO BE GRATEFUL FOR TODAY

"Don't let yesterday's disappointments, overshadow tomorrow's achievements" — Anonymous

Date: /   /

_____

_____

_____

_____

_____

_____

_____

_____

_____

_____

_____

_____

_____

_____

_____

_____

_____

_____

THINGS TO BE GRATEFUL FOR TODAY

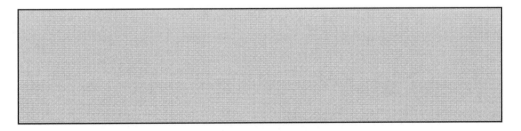

"We are limited, not by our abilities, but by our vision"
— Anonymous

Date: /   /

_____

_____

_____

_____

_____

_____

_____

_____

_____

_____

_____

_____

_____

_____

_____

THINGS TO BE GRATEFUL FOR TODAY

> *"Dreams don't come true. Dreams are true"*
> *— Anonymous*

Date: /   /

THINGS TO BE GRATEFUL FOR TODAY

> *"Happiness is not something you get, but something you do"* — Anonymous

Date: / /

_____

_____
_____
_____
_____
_____
_____
_____
_____
_____
_____
_____
_____
_____
_____
_____
_____

THINGS TO BE GRATEFUL FOR TODAY

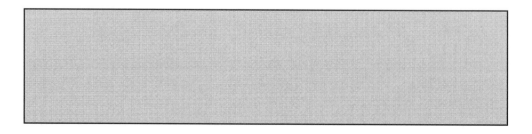

> *"A journey of a thousand miles must begin with a single step."* – Lao Tzu

Date: /   /

_____

_____

_____

_____

_____

_____

_____

_____

_____

_____

_____

_____

_____

_____

_____

_____

THINGS TO BE GRATEFUL FOR TODAY

Date: /   /

THINGS TO BE GRATEFUL FOR TODAY

"You risk more when you don't take any risks"

Date: /   /

_____

_____

_____

_____

_____

_____

_____

_____

_____

_____

_____

_____

_____

_____

_____

_____

THINGS TO BE GRATEFUL FOR TODAY

"A diamond is a chunk of coal that made good under pressure" — Anonymous

Date: /   /

_____

_____

_____

_____

_____

_____

_____

_____

_____

_____

_____

_____

_____

_____

_____

THINGS TO BE GRATEFUL FOR TODAY

> *"No dreamer is ever too small; no dream is ever too big."* — Anonymous

Date: /   /

_____

_____

_____

_____

_____

_____

_____

_____

_____

_____

_____

_____

_____

_____

_____

_____

THINGS TO BE GRATEFUL FOR TODAY

"All our tomorrows depend on today" — *Anonymous*

Date: /   /

_____

_____

_____

_____

_____

_____

_____

_____

_____

_____

_____

_____

_____

_____

_____

THINGS TO BE GRATEFUL FOR TODAY

> *"Remember yesterday, dream of tomorrow, but live for today"* — Anonymous

Date: /   /

THINGS TO BE GRATEFUL FOR TODAY

"Dream is not what you see in sleep, dream is the thing which does not let you sleep" — Anonymous

Date: /   /

_____

_____

_____

_____

_____

_____

_____

_____

_____

_____

_____

_____

_____

THINGS TO BE GRATEFUL FOR TODAY

> *"Don't be pushed by your problems.*
> *Be led by your dreams"* — *Anonymous*

Date: /   /

THINGS TO BE GRATEFUL FOR TODAY

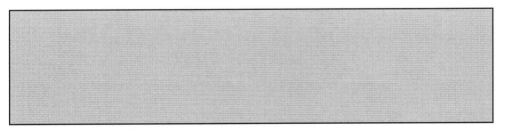

Date: /   /

THINGS TO BE GRATEFUL FOR TODAY

> *"Once you have a dream put all your heart and soul to achieve it"*

Date: /   /

_____

_____

_____

_____

_____

_____

_____

_____

_____

_____

_____

_____

_____

_____

_____

_____

_____

_____

THINGS TO BE GRATEFUL FOR TODAY

Date: / /

_____

_____

_____

_____

_____

_____

_____

_____

_____

_____

_____

_____

_____

_____

_____

_____

_____

THINGS TO BE GRATEFUL FOR TODAY

> *"You create your life by following your dreams with decisive actions"*

Date: /   /

_____

_____

_____

_____

_____

_____

_____

_____

_____

_____

_____

_____

_____

_____

_____

_____

_____

_____

THINGS TO BE GRATEFUL FOR TODAY

Date: /   /

THINGS TO BE GRATEFUL FOR TODAY

"Difficult roads often lead to beautiful destinations"

Date: /   /

_____

_____

_____

_____

_____

_____

_____

_____

_____

_____

_____

_____

_____

_____

_____

_____

_____

_____

THINGS TO BE GRATEFUL FOR TODAY

"The road to success is always full of surprises and temporary failures, real success comes to those who persist"

Date: /   /

_____

_____

_____

_____

_____

_____

_____

_____

_____

_____

_____

_____

_____

_____

_____

_____

THINGS TO BE GRATEFUL FOR TODAY

"Believe in yourself and you will be unstoppable"

Date: /   /

_____

_____

_____

_____

_____

_____

_____

_____

_____

_____

_____

_____

_____

_____

_____

_____

_____

THINGS TO BE GRATEFUL FOR TODAY

> *"Today is another chance to get better"*

Date: /   /

THINGS TO BE GRATEFUL FOR TODAY

> *"To live a creative life, we must lose our fear of being wrong"* - Anonymous

Date: /   /

_____

_____

_____

_____

_____

_____

_____

_____

_____

_____

_____

_____

_____

_____

_____

_____

THINGS TO BE GRATEFUL FOR TODAY

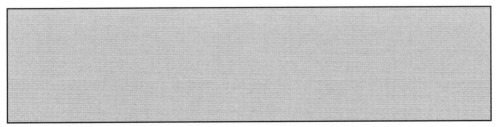

> *"Make each day count, you will never have this day again"*

Date: ___ / ___ / ___

_____

_____

_____

_____

_____

_____

_____

_____

_____

_____

_____

_____

_____

_____

_____

_____

THINGS TO BE GRATEFUL FOR TODAY

> *"If you do what you always did,*
> *you will get what you always got" - Anonymous*

Date: /   /

_____

_____

_____

_____

_____

_____

_____

_____

_____

_____

_____

_____

_____

_____

THINGS TO BE GRATEFUL FOR TODAY

> *"It's not what you look at that matters,*
> *it's what you see"* - Anonymous

Date: /   /

_____
_____
_____
_____
_____
_____
_____
_____
_____
_____
_____
_____
_____
_____
_____
_____

THINGS TO BE GRATEFUL FOR TODAY

"You are capable of amazing things"

Date: /   /

THINGS TO BE GRATEFUL FOR TODAY

"Believe in yourself and you will be unstoppable"

Date: /   /

_____

_____

_____

_____

_____

_____

_____

_____

_____

_____

_____

_____

_____

_____

_____

_____

_____

THINGS TO BE GRATEFUL FOR TODAY

> *"Successful people make a habit of doing what unsuccessful people don't want to do"*
> *— Anonymous*

Date: /   /

THINGS TO BE GRATEFUL FOR TODAY

> *"To be the best you must be able to handle the worst"* - Anonymous

Date: / /

_____

_____

_____

_____

_____

_____

_____

_____

_____

_____

_____

_____

_____

_____

THINGS TO BE GRATEFUL FOR TODAY

"Nothing worth having comes easy" - Anonymous

Date: /   /

THINGS TO BE GRATEFUL FOR TODAY

"Follow your dreams, they know the way"

Date: /   /

THINGS TO BE GRATEFUL FOR TODAY

"Don't Let Anyone Dull Your Sparkle"

Date: /   /

THINGS TO BE GRATEFUL FOR TODAY

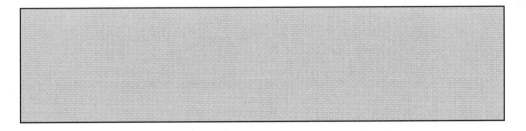

We hope you liked your journal – notebook, please let us know if you liked it by writing a review, it means a lot to us.

Thank you!

DESIGNED BY Creative PositivePress FOR:

CREATIVE JOURNALS FACTORY

FIND OTHER BEAUTIFUL JOURNALS, DIARIES AND NOTEBOOKS AT:

www.CreativeJournalsFactory.com

JOURNALS - DIARIES - NOTEBOOKS - COLORING BOOKS

Manufactured by Amazon.ca
Bolton, ON

20406280R00061